THE
CAREGIVER'S
FINANCIAL
BLUEPRINT

Aging in Place, Saving Money, and Earning Extra Income

ANGELA WILLIS

© Bringing your words to life

Contents

Dedication

My Mother

The woman who led me to Christ at an early age. You not only talked the talk but also walked it. Your gentleness touched many people, but when the Holy Spirit moved you, we saw that boldness come out of you. Even through Dementia, you remained a holy woman. You were my best friend, and it has been an honor to be your caregiver

My Father

My father, you have always been a great provider and a source of stability in my life. Though you have your flaws, your moral integrity has always shone through. You have consistently reminded me to "do what is right," and your unwavering support in all my professional endeavors has been invaluable. Because of your steady presence and the high standards you have set, I hold those same high standards for the men I date. Thank you for being a guiding light and a strong foundation.

Acknowledgments

There are so many people I feel have contributed to my success and staying on the right track thus far. I know that if they had not been supportive, given me words of wisdom, encouraging words, steadfast love, and stability, I would not be the person I am today. I thank God for the people who are out of my life as well. I did not understand it then, but I realize now that I would not have been as open to life, learning new things, and gaining a better perspective on things had they remained in my life. I finally understand it now. As the author of Outliers stated, I feel that it is not about my talent or skills but sometimes just plain luck that some beautiful people have been placed in my life, and I have been given advantages that some other people have not had.

My late Pastor Luberta Brackens

Pastor Luberta Brackens was a great woman of God. My real life "shero." I really believe that there are only a few leaders like you. You were so unselfish and always acknowledged the best in people. You were also a woman full of wisdom and faith in God, my inspiration, and you fed me spiritually time and time again. You are greatly missed.

Pastor Lockett

Pastor Lockett (wherever you are), during the years 2001–2003, you were my "ram in the bush." You were literally an answer to a prayer when I was going through a rough time in my life. I remember it like yesterday: I cried out to God for "help," and that Wednesday night I came to visit Friendship West Baptist Church to watch my cousin get baptized. After the baptism, I decided to stay to hear you teach. Little did I know you were going to teach a series on "Spiritual Warfare," which is what I needed to hear. For years, I kept coming, and through the anointing of God, you would refresh my mind and recharge my spirit every time!

My sister, Andrea

Words cannot describe all that you are and have been to me. Although we fuss, argue, and disagree from time to time, you have always been there. I know that you are a really good person, and whenever I need an opinion, advice, or proofreading on something I am working on, I can always go to you.

Dr. Evelyn Daniels

Dr. Daniels, whom I have not seen in years, you are and were an instrumental woman of God whom I honor and am very glad to have met. I have never had a teacher go beyond and prepare me to face one of the most challenging events I have ever had in my life. You are one individual that I do not want to let down.

There are also a few other people who I would like to thank for helping me write this book. I would like to thank my real estate colleagues up north. You all have shown me so much love, compassion and support in the last year. It was so unexpected, but I am most grateful. Finally, I would like to thank my haters, those who caused me pain, heartbreak, and disappointment. I would not be who I am without you either. Thank you for making me "GROW UP."

Introduction

At thirty-four, I became a Dementia caregiver, which was quite young. My parents had me in their forties, leading to this early responsibility. After college, I worked as a Juvenile Detention Officer. Alongside my full-time job, I was a part-time real estate agent and coordinated community events through my non-profit, Road to Economic Empowerment Enterprises. Essentially, I juggled four roles.

We live in a day where Caregiver burnout is real. The cost associated with caring for someone diagnosed with Dementia or a terminal illness can be expensive. Furthermore, the cost associated with caregiving is not just financial; it is also emotional, mental, physical, and sometimes even spiritual. I remember when I became a Dementia caregiver around 2007. Even though I have a master's in management degree, I struggle with balancing my dual career, personal life, family financial affairs, and care. I was overwhelmed, and I had to get some help fast.

Over the years, my non-profit organization called Road to Economic Empowerment Enterprises has heard endless stories from those overwhelmed with caring for and paying for their terminally ill loved ones' living expenses. As a result, back in 2017, we decided to raise awareness by hosting The Cost of Caregiving: Alzheimer's and Caregivers Financial Health Symposium. The symposium brought in a task force of experts who specialize in the areas of financial and legal planning, elder law, clinical studies, nutrition, veteran's benefits, and other related areas. When we launched The Cost of Caregiving: Alzheimer's and Caregivers Financial Health Symposium, I had no clue the number of lives it would positively impact, including my own.

As a caregiver, entrepreneur with a real estate business and consulting firm, founder of a non-profit, author, community organizer, speaker, and life coach, I share my journey to encourage you. I wrote this book to share my story as a caregiver and to say that caregivers are unsung heroes, whose quiet acts of love and service make a profound difference in the lives of those they care for. Caregiving is not just a ministry but a business as well. The business side is the management of day-to-day affairs, bills, and making sure the person's assets do not run out if the person is still living at home.

Whether you are an employee or a family member looking after a young person with special needs or an elderly person with Dementia or Alzheimer's, this book is for you. According to the Alzheimer's Association, Alzheimer's is the most costly disease a person can have due to the number of doctor visits and emergency visits, long term care, and the demands involved. Sometimes caregivers are forced to choose between retiring early or going into bankruptcy just to keep expenses down. Last year, over a billion hours were spent in unpaid care. According to the Alzheimer's Association, more than five million people have Alzheimer's and other Dementias.

- Approximately two-thirds of caregivers are women, and
- 41 percent of caregivers have a household income of $50,000 or less.
- Approximately one quarter of dementia caregivers are "sandwich generation" caregivers, meaning that they care not only for an aging parent but also for children under the age of 18.

One of my favorite activities is journaling. It is incredibly therapeutic for me. Writing down my feelings and thoughts on paper helps me process and reflect. It's a private conversation between me and God, free from judgment or unsolicited advice. At the end of almost every chapter, there is space for you to journal your thoughts or write notes.

Habakkuk 2:2–3 says, "Write the vision, and make it plain so that those who read may run." I relate to this verse because my vision came together piece by piece. By the end of this book, you will uncover numerous strategies to save money and generate additional income by identifying your niche. You will explore valuable resources and support systems to guide you on your journey, discover methods to ease tensions among family members, and learn how to safeguard your energy. If you're ready for the challenge, let's dive in.

About Me and How I Became a Caregiver

I was born and raised in Dallas, Texas. My mother was a stay-at-home wife and mom, but she also had her own in-home daycare. My father was an aircraft mechanic for forty years with Aviall Services, now G.E. Services. Growing up, I was a shy, skinny girl who loved church. I would sing in the mirror, holding a candle as my microphone. I participated in the Sunbeam choir as a child. As I got older, I joined the Sweet Fellowship mass choir for a while. I led a couple songs. People were shocked when I came out of my shyness to sing 'grown up gospel songs,' but I loved the Lord. I felt God pulling at me when I was very young. I accepted Christ into my life at the age of twelve.

I had some growing pains, but I lived a comfortable middle-class life. Since I was sixteen years old, I have always written down my goals. Early on, I remember wanting to be a gospel singer and nutritionist. After graduating high school, I wanted to go to college and study business. I later changed my major to criminal justice. After graduating with my bachelor's in criminal justice, I became a juvenile detention officer. A couple of years later, I obtained my real estate license and founded Road to Economic Empowerment Enterprises, a 501(c)(3) non-profit. When my parents were diagnosed with dementia and their health started to decline, my life began to revolve around them. Honestly, I am a different person because of it.

As I mentioned earlier, at thirty-four, I became a Dementia Caregiver. I did not choose to be a caregiver, but it sort of fell on me because I was living at home with my elderly parents, who had me in their forties. Someone once asked me if I was running a group home. In a sense, that is what it felt like. My mother was the first to be diagnosed with dementia in 2007. Back then, there was not much support or information about how to care for someone diagnosed with Dementia or Alzheimer's. Yes, there was tons of research, but not much information on how to be a good caregiver. Today, there is a lot of information about both found in books and training for Dementia and Alzheimer's Caregivers but not much in 2007. I learned how to be a good caregiver through hands on training. I also learned through trial and error.

I really and truly believe that there is no one way of dealing with a person who is diagnosed with Alzheimer's or Dementia. Yes, they will have similar symptoms, but your loved one or client is an individual, and you must learn how to communicate with and care for them on an individual basis. Dementia and Alzheimer's can take a person down so many different avenues. My mother never had seizures before the diagnosis, but as the disease progressed, she began having them.

My mother was diagnosed with Vascular Dementia in 2007, and my father was diagnosed around 2015, maybe earlier. We took my mother to all kinds of specialists, beginning with her primary doctor. She then had the EEG probe test, where they glued EKG probes to her head. She went to see a neurologist and later went back to a primary doctor, who diagnosed her with Vascular Dementia.

I was in denial at first. In the beginning, my mother would tell me that she could not remember certain things, and I would be like, You got to combat that fear with the word of God. I didn't want to accept what was happening. I later accepted the diagnosis and started learning what I could.

My mother fought the disease from roughly 2007 up until January 5, 2021. I later learned that Dementia and Alzheimer's are also defined differently. Dementia is an umbrella of all kinds of illnesses, such as Lewy bodies, Parkinson's, etc. It can branch out into Alzheimer's. The home health industry was different too. Once my mother started to become more confused and less easy to deal with it, we hired a private home health caregiver to assist me. Back then, you could really get good quality professional help, and they would stay with the company for years. It seemed like caregivers really took their jobs seriously.

As the home health industry began to boom, finding good help was like finding a needle in a haystack. The turnover rate became high in the home health industry. Over the years, we have probably had over twenty caregivers. Some of these include caregivers from home health and private-paid caregivers from Care.com. I have friends who own their own home health companies, and the answer is the same – the turnover is high in the home health industry.

Small business owners are often faced with making a profit, and to make a profit, they have to offer almost the minimum wage or split the profits. Part-time employees are also usually in charge of finding their own health insurance. Before I go too far, I will disclose that we have tried both the nursing home, memory care, group home, and home health. No matter where we went, it seemed like only a handful of people took pride in their work. I think that is the case everywhere, regardless of what your occupation is.

What It Means to Be a Caregiver

I really don't think a person can write it all in one book about what it is like to be a long-term caregiver for someone who is terminally ill and with a mental declining health condition. There are joys and pains in caregiving. I can never say it enough that it is also "work." It is a sacrifice at times. I can remember the day when my stomach became inflamed due to being under chronic stress. I was already working the night shift, which is stressful on the body as it is, but I was also caring for my mother. She started having seizures out of nowhere.

Caring for someone with a debilitating disease like Alzheimer's can be one of the most stressful roles a person could have. Especially when you do not feel like you get enough support. It is also like working a second job. In my case, I had two parents diagnosed with Dementia. One parent was totally dependent. She lost her ability to talk, walk, and communicate her needs before she passed away in 2021. Whenever she did not feel well, we had to troubleshoot and find the issue. What makes it harder being a caregiver is when you have to make all the decisions as it pertains to your loved one's health and financial affairs because they may not have discussed it or put anything in writing or verbally expressed should they become incapacitated, incoherent, or incompetent about what their wishes are.

Again, there are joys and pains in caregiving. I see it as a privilege, an honor, and a ministry sometimes. Then there are days when I want to run away. My sister, Andrea, and I knew Alzheimer's was a detrimental disease, but no one told us that our mother would start having seizures. No one told us that she would forget how to walk, and we would have to re-teach her how to walk again. No one told us would fight with doctors at her nursing home about conducting labs just to stay on top of her UTIs. No one told us we would get little support from social workers, doctors, and the so-called medical team. No one told me that my social life would be non-existent for years.

Being my parents' caregiver has literally changed my life. It was something I was not prepared for but inherited due to living with them. Nor did I know that much about Dementia or Alzheimer's when my mother was diagnosed in 2007. I knew that it was incurable and resulted in death. In my opinion, no one knows all the mysteries of Dementia and Alzheimer's. When my mother was diagnosed, I was told the average life span for someone living with Alzheimer's was about ten years. My mother lived with the disease for about fourteen years. The main drugs when my mother was diagnosed were Namenda, Aricept, and the Exelon patch. There is still no cure for Alzheimer's. Some people decline slowly, and some decline right away. It helps to have family and supporters, but there is still no absolute way of being prepared for the emotional toll it can take. I remember years ago: I started venting to my mother about how my social life was just non-existent, and she retorted, "You think I asked for this?" I shut up real fast because I failed to think about how she felt.

Many people think being a Dementia caregiver is not that difficult. In the beginning, that might be true because the person who is diagnosed may be able to still make decisions and may not need that much attention. However, as the person lives longer, it is only a matter of time before they will require more assistance. And the longer a person lives, the more expensive it can get. For this chapter, I have decided to break it down into different parts on what it means to be a long-term Dementia Caregiver.

At its core, caregiving is an act of love. It involves putting the needs of another person above your own and making sacrifices to ensure their well-being. Caregivers often find themselves in this role out of a deep sense of duty and affection, whether it be for a parent, spouse, child, or friend. Caregiving also requires compassion and empathy. A caregiver must possess an abundance of compassion and empathy. Understanding the struggles and pain of the person they are caring for requires putting themselves in other people's shoes. This deep emotional connection allows caregivers to provide not just physical support but also emotional and psychological comfort.

Caregiving requires patience and resilience. It is not a sprint; it is a marathon. The daily challenges can be overwhelming, from managing medications and appointments to assisting with basic needs like bathing and eating. Patience becomes a cornerstone virtue, allowing caregivers to navigate the ups and downs without losing hope or becoming frustrated. Resilience is equally important, helping caregivers bounce back from the inevitable setbacks and maintain their strength over the long haul.

Caregiving is often physically demanding. There were times when me and my sister's backs would be hurting because we often had to bend over to change our mother's linens or help pull her up out of bed, etc. Even using a gait belt, we still had back soreness. Depending on the level of care required, caregivers might need to assist with mobility, manage medical equipment, or provide hands-on care. This physical toll can be exhausting, and it's crucial for caregivers to recognize the importance of self-care to avoid burnout.

Caregiving requires a great deal of organizational skills. The better you are at managing tasks and responsibilities, the less stress you can have. Caregivers frequently juggle numerous responsibilities, from coordinating medical appointments, running errands, and managing finances to ensuring the home environment is safe and accessible. Effective time management and prioritization are essential to handling these tasks efficiently.

Caregiving can be an emotional rollercoaster. The bond between caregiver and care recipient deepens, but so does the potential for emotional strain. Feelings of frustration, sadness, and even guilt are common as caregivers grapple with the challenges and their limitations.

Caregiving can be very stressful. It is essential for caregivers to find healthy ways to cope with stress and anxiety. Support groups, therapy, and journaling can be valuable outlets for expressing emotions and finding solace. Connecting with others who share similar experiences can provide a sense of community and understanding.

Finding Meaning and Purpose

Caregiving can be a profound spiritual journey. The act of selflessly caring for another person can deepen one's understanding of love, compassion, and the human spirit. It provides an opportunity to live out values and beliefs in a tangible and impactful way. For many caregivers, spirituality plays a significant role in their journey. Turning to faith can offer strength, guidance, and a sense of purpose. Whether through prayer, meditation, or other spiritual practices, caregivers often find solace and inspiration in their beliefs. In the midst of the challenges, it's important to celebrate the small victories. Each step forward, no matter how minor it may seem, is a testament to the caregiver's dedication and the progress of the care recipient. These moments of joy and accomplishment provide motivation and reinforce the value of the caregiver's efforts.

Being a caregiver is a complex, rewarding, and at times challenging role. It requires a unique blend of compassion, resilience, and dedication. The journey of caregiving is not just about providing physical support; it is about offering emotional and spiritual sustenance as well. Caregivers are unsung heroes whose quiet acts of love and service make a profound difference in the lives of those they care for. Understanding and embracing the essence of being a caregiver can lead to a more fulfilling and meaningful experience for both the caregiver and the care recipient.

Now, it's your turn. In the space provided, write out your thoughts on what being a caregiver or caretaker means to you.

_____

_____

_____

_____

_____

_____

_____

_____

_____

_____

_____

_____

_____

_____

_____

_____

_____

_____

_____

_____

_____

_____

_____

The Cost of Caregiving
Financial Health Symposium

Organizing and planning community outreach initiatives come naturally to me because I have been organizing outreach events through my nonprofit organization, Road to Economic Empowerment Enterprises, for years. In the beginning, we offered homebuyer seminars. We later expanded our programs to include financial literacy and mental health wellness. Overwhelmed as a caregiver and lacking support from friends and family in 2017, I decided to host a symposium with guest speakers to address various aspects of caregiving. They discussed the signs of Alzheimer's, the importance of financial and legal planning, nutrition, self-care, and available resources for caregivers. I named it "The Cost of Caregiving: Alzheimer's and Caregivers Financial Health Symposium."

Before I dive deeper, Road to Economic Empowerment Enterprises, a 501(c)(3) non-profit organization, collaborates with the business community to deliver professional and personal development opportunities in financial literacy, entrepreneurship, and affordable housing education. Often likened to SCORE with a financial twist, our mission is clear: "Providing strategies on building wealth and reshaping the culture for those living in underserved communities." Since 2006, we have empowered communities in Dallas County, promoting financial literacy, entrepreneurship, and mental health wellness through dedicated outreach and event planning.

At R2EE Enterprises, we believe that in order to have more economic empowerment, we must be proactive and intentional about (1) improving our financial literacy, (2) mental health wellness, and (3) reshaping the culture by empowering our youth on how to become leaders and culture change agents through entrepreneurship. We also believe that in order to achieve more economic empowerment, we must work together, master our mindset, be disciplined in our spending, and focus on becoming owners versus renters.

When I launched "The Cost of Caregiving: Alzheimer's and Caregivers Financial Health Symposium," I did not know it would positively impact so many lives, including my own. I simply did it due to being a caregiver for over ten years with little support. I am not an expert at being a caregiver, but what I do know as a result of those ten years is that *no one can do it alone*. No one can live with the disease alone, and you definitely cannot fight it alone. It takes a team of the right people to make life a little easier when dealing with Dementia and Alzheimer's.

Now, it's your turn. In the space provided write out your thoughts on how much you think long term care cost and how much you would pay for long term care.

_____

_____

_____

_____

_____

_____

_____

_____

_____

_____

_____

_____

_____

_____

_____

_____

_____

_____

_____

_____

_____

_____

_____

_____

_____

The Importance of Self Care

In the demanding role of a caregiver, it is easy to overlook one's own needs in the process of taking care of others. However, neglecting self-care can lead to burnout, emotional exhaustion, and physical health problems. This chapter explores the critical importance of self-care for caregivers, offering practical strategies and insights to maintain well-being while providing care.

Understanding Self-Care

Self-care is the practice of taking action to preserve or improve one's own health and well-being. It encompasses a wide range of activities that promote physical, emotional, and mental health. For caregivers, self-care is not a luxury but a necessity, ensuring they have the strength and resilience to provide effective care.

Physical Self-Care

Physical self-care involves maintaining your body through healthy habits. This includes getting adequate sleep, eating nutritious meals, staying hydrated, and engaging in regular physical activity.

- Sleep: Quality sleep is essential for physical health and mental clarity. Caregivers should aim for 7-9 hours of sleep per night and establish a consistent sleep routine.

- Nutrition: A balanced diet fuels the body and mind. Caregivers should prioritize meals rich in fruits, vegetables, whole grains, and lean proteins while limiting processed foods and sugars.

- Exercise: Regular physical activity reduces stress, boosts mood, and improves overall health. Even short, daily walks or stretching exercises can make a significant difference.

Emotional Self-Care

Emotional self-care focuses on managing emotions and finding healthy outlets for stress and frustration.

- Journaling: Writing down thoughts and feelings can provide clarity and emotional release.

- Mindfulness and Meditation: Practices such as mindfulness and meditation can help caregivers stay present and manage stress more effectively.

- Seeking Support: Talking to friends, family, or support groups can provide emotional relief and a sense of community.

Mental Self-Care

Mental self-care involves activities that stimulate the mind and provide a break from caregiving duties.

- Hobbies: Engaging in hobbies or activities that you enjoy can provide a much-needed mental break.

- Learning: Continuing education or learning new skills can keep the mind sharp and provide a sense of accomplishment.

- Relaxation Techniques: Practices such as deep breathing, progressive muscle relaxation, or yoga can help reduce mental stress.

Barriers to Self-Care

Despite its importance, caregivers often face barriers to practicing self-care. Understanding and addressing these obstacles can help caregivers prioritize their well-being.

Guilt

Many caregivers feel guilty for taking time for themselves, believing it detracts from the care they provide. It is crucial to recognize that self-care is not selfish; it is necessary for sustainable caregiving.

Time Constraints

The demands of caregiving can make it difficult to find time for self-care. Caregivers can overcome this by scheduling regular self-care activities and seeking respite care or support from others.

Lack of Support

Some caregivers may feel isolated and lack support. Building a network of friends, family, and professional resources can provide the necessary support for self-care.

Practical Self-Care Strategies

Implementing self-care does not have to be complicated or time-consuming. Here are some practical strategies caregivers can integrate into their daily routines:

- Set Boundaries: Clearly define your limits and communicate them to others. Learn to say no when necessary to prevent overextending yourself.

- Create a Routine: Establish a daily routine that includes time for self-care activities. Consistency can help make self-care a habit.

- Delegate Tasks: Do not hesitate to delegate tasks to others. Accept help from family, friends, or professional caregivers to lighten your load.

- Take Breaks: Regular breaks throughout the day can help you recharge. Even a few minutes of downtime can make a significant difference.

- Practice Gratitude: Focus on the positives by keeping a gratitude journal or taking time each day to reflect on things you are thankful for.

The Benefits of Self-Care

The benefits of self-care extend beyond the caregiver, positively impacting the care recipient and the overall caregiving dynamic.

- Improved Health: Regular self-care leads to better physical and mental health, reducing the risk of burnout and illness.

- Enhanced Resilience: Caregivers who practice self-care are more resilient and better equipped to handle the challenges of caregiving.

- Better Care: When caregivers are healthy and well-rested, they can provide higher quality care.

- Positive Role Modeling: Practicing self-care sets a positive example for others, demonstrating the importance of maintaining one's well-being.

Self-care is an essential component of effective caregiving. By prioritizing their own well-being, caregivers can maintain the physical, emotional, and mental strength needed to provide compassionate and competent care. Embracing self-care is not only beneficial for caregivers but also enhances the overall caregiving experience, ensuring that both the caregiver and the care recipient thrive.

Now, it's your turn. In the space provided write down some self-care practices you are going to take or take already.

_____

_____

_____

_____

_____

_____

_____

_____

_____

_____

_____

_____

_____

_____

_____

_____

_____

_____

_____

_____

_____

_____

Reducing the Friction Among Family Members Surrounding Money

Finances can put a strain on any relationship, even family. People often feel tension when there is a shift in family dynamics or when they have to adjust to a "New Normal." One of the best ways to keep friction down is to be open and upfront about your wishes. Honest communication is the cornerstone of reducing friction. According to Jeremiah 29:11, God has a plan and purpose for each of us, even when we may not understand it. It is essential to recognize that everything happens for a reason and there is a time and a season for everything. In each season of our lives, we must understand that elder law, estate planning, and financial planning are crucial when leaving behind a legacy and to help reduce friction. Establishing your wishes through legal measures such as assigning a power of attorney, creating a will, and setting up a trust can help minimize family conflicts if you experience a decline in mental or physical health.

Here are some tips to foster open dialogue

- Regular Updates: Keep family members informed about financial decisions, changes in your parent's financial status, and any significant expenditures. Regular updates can be shared through family meetings, emails, or group chats.

- Transparency: Be transparent about your actions and decisions. Share relevant documents, receipts, and bank statements to build trust and demonstrate that you are managing your finances responsibly.

- Listen Actively: Encourage family members to express their concerns and opinions. Listen actively and empathetically, showing that you value their input and are willing to address their worries.

Establishing Clear Boundaries

Define clear boundaries regarding the extent of your authority and the involvement of other family members. This can help prevent misunderstandings and conflicts. Consider the following steps:

- Define Roles: Clearly outline the roles and responsibilities of each family member in the caregiving and financial management processes. This can include decision-making, day-to-day management, and oversight.

- Set Limits: Establish what decisions you can make independently, and which ones require family consensus. For significant financial decisions, such as selling property or making large investments, seek input from all concerned parties.

Seeking Professional Guidance

Engaging professionals can help mitigate conflicts and ensure sound financial management:

- Financial Advisors: Consult with a financial advisor to develop a comprehensive financial plan for your parents. An advisor can provide objective guidance and help you make informed decisions.

- Legal Counsel: Work with an attorney to understand the legal implications of your role and ensure compliance with relevant laws and regulations. An attorney can also mediate disputes if they arise.

- Mediators: In cases of significant conflict, consider hiring a mediator to facilitate discussions and help resolve disagreements. Mediators are trained to manage family dynamics and can provide a neutral perspective.

Documenting Decisions

Keeping detailed records of all financial transactions and decisions is essential for accountability and transparency:

- Maintain Records: Keep meticulous records of all financial activities, including receipts, invoices, bank statements, and investment documents. Organize these records in a way that is accessible to other family members if needed.

- Create Reports: Regularly create financial reports summarizing income, expenses, and significant financial decisions. Share these reports with family members to keep them informed and involved.

Respecting Your Parents' Wishes

Respecting your parents' wishes and autonomy is crucial to maintaining family harmony:

- Discuss Preferences: Have open discussions with your parents about their financial preferences and goals. Understand their priorities and ensure your decisions align with their wishes.

- Involve Your Parent: Involve your parent in financial discussions and decisions as much as possible. This can help them feel valued and respected, reducing potential conflicts.

Although these suggestions may help reduce friction, they do not eliminate it altogether. Managing a parent's finances as a caregiver with power of attorney can be challenging, but by fostering open communication, establishing clear boundaries, seeking professional guidance, documenting decisions, and respecting your parent's wishes, you can significantly reduce friction and maintain family harmony. Remember, your role is not just about managing finances but also about ensuring your parents' well-being and preserving family relationships.

CHAPTER 6

Ways to Save Money

Sometimes it's not about making money but about saving. Over the past year, I have helped my parents save over $20k in home repairs. Every little bit counts when you live on a fixed income. I have had many caregiver assistants come and go. When I got my master's degree in management, I knew I would hire people to work for me, but I never thought about the home health arena. Being a competent caregiver involves work. In the beginning, I had pretty good caregivers who assisted me in cooking, conducting household duties, and providing companionship to my parents. But today, finding a good assistant caregiver or a good assisted/nursing home is like trying to find a needle in a haystack. So many people do not want to work. On the other hand, I knew a lot of caregivers or nurse aides that were good at what they did but were not motivated due to the salary (so they say). But I have paid good money for a caregiver, and the output was just about the same. Due to the rising cost of medical and care expenses, it is important to be aware of the programs that are out there that can help you save money.

States can offer a variety of services under the State Plan Home and Community Based Services (HCBS) benefit. People must meet state-defined criteria based on need and typically receive a combination of acute-care medical services (such as dental and skilled nursing services) and long-term services (such as respite, case management, supported employment, and environmental modifications) in home and community-based settings. Texas Health and Human Services also offers a program called "In-Home Care." You can call 1-888-337-6377 or go to your state Department of Health and Human Services, formerly known as the Department of Aging and Disability (DADS), and search for programs and funding for various in-home services, residential facilities, respite, and community-based services.

Veterans Aid and Attendance Pension

The Aid and Attendance Pension Benefit is another program available in Texas that can be used to pay family members to provide care. It is important to note that this program exclusively applies to war-time veterans or their surviving spouses who need help with their daily activities. The program does not pay spouses or children for their caregiving roles. How it works is extremely complicated. The paperwork is very tedious, and I highly advise you to use a Veterans Service Officer or Representative to help you get the process started. Once the veteran receives approval for aid and attendance, a field service officer will inspect the veteran's home to determine your eligibility as an appointed fiduciary. Once appointed, you must set up a fiduciary bank account to prevent co-mingling funds. You must also have a budget and keep a paper trail of every dime you spend, because they will audit you every year or at any time. Therefore, it is crucial to maintain a high level of organization. Veteran's Administration: 1-800-827-1000 or www.va.gov

Long-Term Care Insurance

Long-term insurance is a privately issued insurance policy that covers the cost of nursing home care, assisted living, and home health care. Premiums are based on age, health, length of deductible periods, amount paid, and duration of benefits. You can also use it to hire family members as caregivers. According to Bill Baldwin on Forbes, he thinks long-term insurance has its advantages and disadvantages. For example, the insurance company has the ability to raise the cost later in life. Baldwin suggests planning on using your home equity to fund your elder care or putting your money in a fixed deferred annuity (what is often called a longevity annuity that you buy in your 60s). I looked into getting long-term care insurance for myself, but I do not like how it works.

Area Agency on Aging

You can't make money with the Area Agency on Aging, but they can help you save money and be a resource, especially if you are a caregiver for an elderly person. I am not sure if every state has a local chapter, but I would suggest that you call 211, 311, or visit the National Association of Area Agencies on Aging for a chapter in a major city near you. There is a chapter in Dallas, Texas, and they have previously helped us save money on repairs. One of my seminars featured a representative promoting their programs.

The Dallas Area Agency on Aging receives funding from various sources and offers an array of services. To my knowledge, they are not an income-based program like others. You don't need a certain income to get services. Those services include counseling and support groups, such as Medicare assistance, respite care, minor home repairs, education and training, and supplemental services. You can also try the Eldercare Locator at 1-800-677-1116.US Administration on Aging information on local programs: www.eldercare.gov/Eldercare.NET/Public/Index.aspx

Other programs may exist, but I've used these and included more resources at the end of this book.

Ways to Make an Additional Income

Finances can be stressful. As I mentioned earlier, caregiving has a business side. In fact, caregivers must play different roles and often-times wear many hats just to save money. For instance, if you are a caregiver for an individual who is still living at home and is completely dependent or co-dependent, your daily responsibilities may include acting as a nurse, CNA, social worker, handyman, property manager, answering service, activity director, private chef, housekeeper, land-scaper, gardener, security guard, accountant, secretary, tax preparer, contractor, employer, minister, and so on. Being a caregiver is hard work. Do you see all of these trades and jobs within yourself? If you are trying to make an extra income, the first thing you need to do is recognize the gifts you have inside of you. Ask yourself right now, "What am I good at?" What comes naturally to me?

A good place to start is by determining your SMART goals. SMART is an acronym that stands for Specific, Measurable, Assignable, Realistic, and Time-Related. Some authors say the acronym stands for Specific, Measurable, Achievable, Realistic, and Timely.

Aging in Place: SMART Goals

First of all, let's define what a SMART goal is. We use SMART Goals as a framework to formulate specific, measurable, achievable, rele-vant, and time-bound objectives. This approach helps us to clarify goals and enhance the chances of successful completion.

As a caregiver, setting SMART goals can help you stay focused and track your progress. Here are some examples:

- Specific: "I will help my aging parent improve their mobility by assisting with daily exercises."

- Measurable: "I will track my parents' progress by recording the number of steps they can take each day using a pedometer."

- Achievable: "I will gradually increase the exercise intensity to ensure it's manageable and safe for my parents."

- Relevant: "Improving mobility is important because it will enhance my parent's overall quality of life and reduce the risk of falls."

- Time-bound: "I will achieve a 20% increase in my parent's daily steps within three months."

Remember to adapt these SMART goals to the specific needs and capabilities of the person you are caring for. Regularly assess and adjust your goals as the caregiving situation evolves.

Ways to Make an Additional Income: Finding Your Niche and Creating a Side Hustle

R2EE Assessment

A good place to discover what your niche is by writing down what you are good at. This is not the definitive method for identifying your talents or strengths, but it serves as a starting point. Of course, there are better assessments out there, but again, this is just a foundation to get you thinking and moving in the right direction.

What Am I Good At?

Am I good at serving others?

Am I good at communicating?

Am I good at finances, math, or computers?

Am I good at working with kids?

Am I good at shopping?

Am I good at multi-tasking?

Am I good at drawing or designing?

Am I good at proofreading or editing?

Am I good at ghostwriting or posting things on social media?

Am I good at problem-solving or fixing things?

Am I good at baking or cooking?

Do I love pets?

Strengths/Talents	Side Hustles
1. Serving Others	UberEats/Cleaning Services/Support Type Service
2. Communicator	Sales/Secretary/Real Estate
3. Math, Finances, or Computer	Financial Planner/Accountant/Teacher/Coding
4. Working with kids	Babysitter/Online Tutoring/children books
5. Shopping/SALES	E-commerce online store ex: amazon, shopify, etsy
6. Multi-tasking	Project manager/event planner/moving company
7. Proofreader or editing	Video editor/proofreader
8. NOTARY	NOTARY SERVICE
9. Ghostwriting or posting things on social media	Entertainment Blog/Journalist/Podcaster
10. Problem Solving/Fixing things/working on cars	Creating a program/setting up financial software/installing tv mounts/Handyman Service/Mobile Detailer
11. Cooking	Baker/private chef
12. Pet Lover	Pet sitting/dog walker

Now, it's your turn. In the space provided, write down your SMART Goals.

_____

_____

_____

_____

_____

_____

_____

_____

_____

_____

_____

_____

_____

_____

_____

_____

_____

_____

_____

_____

_____

_____

CHAPTER 8

More Ways to Make an Additional Income: Using Your Home

Renting out a room or converting a second home into a rental property is another option you could consider bringing in extra income if you or the person receiving care is still somewhat independent and needs very little care or supervision. This idea is a much more complicated process because things can go wrong extremely fast. If you belong to Generation X or older, you likely recall the television series "The Golden Girls," which featured Betty White, Bea Arthur, Rue McClanahan, and Estelle Getty. "Golden Girls" is an American sitcom that is about four women ranging in their fifties and up who co-lived together in a nice home in Miami. They develop a close friendship and bond. Most people think co-housing and co-living are the same thing, but they are not. Co-housing is more like a duplex or multi-unit situation where each individual, couple, or family has an independent living unit. Consider condos, apartments, or single-family homes as examples. Residents share spaces outside of their homes. These spaces include game rooms, commercial kitchens, pools, meeting rooms, and fitness rooms, among others.

Co-living is where people without family ties cohabitate in a single dwelling. Each resident typically has a private bedroom (or a bedroom and bathroom), but they share other rooms such as the dining room, family room, kitchen, and sunroom. Like anything, there are pros and cons to co-living. The advantages of co-living include saving money by dividing up utility, maintenance, and rent costs. It can also help combat loneliness. On the other hand, co-living can be a nightmare if you don't complement each other.

To help reduce conflicts, make a written agreement outlining who pays for what, when, and how bills will be divided. Reach an agreement on clutter and messiness. Outline a policy on pets and guests before specific situations arise. For example, how often or for how long can residents entertain guests? If you like a lot of privacy, address any concerns upfront about how much space you need and what is off limits. Discuss any allergies, physical limitations, or lifestyle preferences. Look for someone who is financially stable, shares some of your interests, and has a similar lifestyle. Find out whether they travel a lot for work or work from home. Try a trial period of two weeks to see how well everyone gets along. Most importantly, include the person on the lease if renting. Consider having a realtor or an attorney devise a contract.

Should you decide to open your home, I highly recommend conducting a thorough interview, a background check on a person of the same gender, and a credit check. Meet potential roommates for the first time in a public place. If you do like them and want to show the home, make sure to have a friend or family member at your place when you invite a potential roommate over for the first time. Get references from previous roommates. You can find roommates on websites like Silvernest.com, Roommates4Boomers.com (women only), Home-ShareVermont.org, Roommate Network, and Seattle-based Housing Connector.

I just gave you more than ten side hustles you can do. You can customize these businesses around your schedule. If none of these questions match your skills, I suggest you get on YouTube and get ideas. YouTube is a cost-effective resource that offers a wealth of videos on DIY projects, strategies, current trends, and side hustles. They have an enormous amount of content. Another place you can go for an in-depth skills test analysis is a non-profit organization like the DEC Network or a community college. You can also pay to do an assessment with platforms like "The Strength Finder's Test," created by Tom Rath. You can even read books like the "Occupational Outlook Handbook" by the Bureau of Labor Statistics.

Now, it's your turn. In the space provided, write down what your strengths are.

_____

_____

_____

_____

_____

_____

_____

_____

_____

_____

_____

_____

_____

_____

_____

_____

_____

_____

_____

_____

_____

CHAPTER 9

Aging in Place Strategies

I know some of you may be asking, "What is Aging in Place?" Aging in place refers to the idea of staying in one's own home and community safely, comfortably, and independently as one gets older. Here are some strategies and considerations to help achieve this:

1. Home Modifications: Make the necessary changes to your home to improve safety and accessibility. This may include installing handrails, ramps, grab bars, and non-slip flooring.

2. Technology: Explore assistive technologies like medical alert systems, home automation, and smart devices that can help with daily tasks and provide peace of mind for both the elderly person and their caregivers.

3. Medical Care: Set up a reliable healthcare team and consider home healthcare services when needed. Regular medical check-ups and medication management are crucial.

4. Social Support: Encourage social interaction and maintain a support network. Loneliness and isolation can be significant issues for seniors, so staying connected with family and friends is important.

5. Transportation: Ensure access to reliable transportation for medical appointments, grocery shopping, and other essential activities. Consider community or volunteer transportation services.

6. Financial Planning: Plan for the financial aspects of aging in place. This may involve budgeting for future healthcare expenses and understanding Medicare or other insurance coverage.

7. Legal and Estate Planning: Ensure that legal documents such as wills, powers of attorney, and advance healthcare directives are in place. This helps with decision-making and asset management.

8. In-Home Care: If necessary, arrange for in-home care services, including personal care aides or nurses who can provide assistance with daily tasks.

9. Fall Prevention: Falls are a common concern for seniors. Remove tripping hazards, use non-slip mats, and consider wearing appropriate footwear to prevent falls.

10. Nutrition and Exercise: Maintain a healthy diet and exercise routine. This can help with overall well-being and mobility.

11. Emergency Preparedness: Have a plan for emergencies, including a communication plan with family members, a list of important contacts, and emergency supplies.

12. Regular Assessments: Continuously assess the living situation to adapt to changing needs. What works for an elderly person today may need adjustment in the future.

13. Home Security: Invest in a reliable home security system for added safety.

14. Supportive Services: Look into local senior centers, organizations, and support groups that can provide resources and social opportunities for seniors.

15. Professional Guidance: Consult with professionals such as geriatric care managers or aging-in-place specialists for personalized guidance.

Aging in place requires careful planning and ongoing adjustments to ensure a safe and comfortable environment as one grows older. Each individual's needs and circumstances are unique, so it's important to tailor these strategies to specific situations.

Now, it's your turn. In the space provided, what are some "Aging in Place Strategies" you are going to start doing

_____

_____

_____

_____

_____

_____

_____

_____

_____

_____

_____

_____

_____

_____

_____

_____

_____

_____

_____

_____

_____

_____

Aging in Place:
SMART PLAN

In this chapter, I would like to talk about what an Aging in Place SMART PLAN is and how to put one together. Creating a smart plan for caregivers involves several key steps:

Assess the Care Recipient's Needs: Start by evaluating the physical, emotional, and medical needs of the person you're caring for. Consider their daily routines, medical conditions, and any special requirements.

- Set Clear Goals: Define your caregiving goals. Are you providing temporary care or long-term support? Be specific about what you hope to achieve.

- Create a Schedule: Establish a daily or weekly caregiving schedule. Include time for personal breaks and self-care to prevent burnout.

- Build a Support Network: Reach out to family, friends, or support groups who can assist you. Don't hesitate to ask for help when needed.

- Medical and Legal Planning: Ensure you have access to the person's medical information, legal documents (such as a power of attorney or living will), and contact details for healthcare providers.

- Financial Planning: Understand the financial aspects of caregiving. This includes budgeting, managing expenses, and exploring financial assistance options if necessary.

- Safety Precautions: Identify potential safety hazards in the care-giving environment and take steps to mitigate them.

- Emotional Well-Being: Caregiving can be emotionally challenging. Seek emotional support, practice self-care, and consider counseling or therapy if needed.

- Education and Training: If you are caring for someone with a specific medical condition, seek relevant training and education to provide better care.

- Regular Check-ins: Keep regular communication with the care recipient's healthcare team.

- Document and Track: Maintain records of medications, doctor's appointments, and any changes in the care recipient's condition.

- Plan for Contingencies: Have a backup plan in case you are unable to provide care temporarily. This might involve respite care or backup caregivers.

- Adapt and Reassess: As the person's needs change, be ready to make adjustments.

Now, it's your turn. In the space provided, write down your SMART Plan of Action.

_____

_____

_____

_____

_____

_____

_____

_____

_____

_____

_____

_____

_____

_____

_____

_____

_____

_____

_____

_____

_____

The Financial Blueprint

Creating a financial blueprint for caregivers involves outlining a comprehensive plan to manage finances effectively while considering the unique challenges and responsibilities associated with caregiving. Here's a step-by-step guide to developing this blueprint:

- Financial Blueprint for Caregivers

- Assess your current Financial Situation

- Income Sources: List all sources of income (salary, side jobs, government assistance).

- Expenses: Track monthly expenses (housing, utilities, food, transportation, healthcare, personal care, and miscellaneous).

- Debt: Identify outstanding debts (credit cards, loans).

- Savings: Evaluate current savings and emergency funds.

Set Financial Goals

- Short-Term Goals: Emergency fund, debt repayment, monthly savings.

- Long-Term Goals: Retirement savings, college fund for children, purchasing a home.

Create a Budget

- Income and Expenses: Use the income and expenses list to create a monthly budget.
- Allocation: Allocate funds for necessary expenses and set aside a portion for savings and debt repayment.

Manage Debt

- Consolidate: Consider consolidating debt for a lower interest rate.
- Repayment Plan: Set up a repayment plan that prioritizes high-interest debts.
- Avoid New Debt: Limit new debt and use credit wisely.

Build an Emergency Fund

- Savings Target: Aim for 3-6 months' worth of living expenses.
- Automatic Transfers: Set up automatic transfers to a dedicated savings account.

Plan for Retirement

- Contributions: Contribute regularly to retirement accounts (401(k), IRA).
- Employer Match: Take full advantage of employer matching programs.
- Invest Wisely: Consider a diversified investment portfolio.

Insurance Coverage

- Health Insurance: Ensure adequate health insurance coverage.
- Disability Insurance: Consider disability insurance for income protection.
- Life Insurance: Secure life insurance to protect dependents.

Take advantage of Tax Benefits

- Tax Deductions: Explore tax deductions and credits related to caregiving.
- Flexible Spending Accounts (FSA): Utilize FSAs for healthcare and dependent care expenses.

Seek Financial Assistance Programs

- Government Programs: Research and apply for available government assistance programs.
- Non-Profit Organizations: Look into non-profits offering financial aid for caregivers.

Continuously Monitor and Adjust

- Regular Reviews: Review the financial situation and budget regularly.
- Adjust Goals: As circumstances change, adjust financial goals.
- Seek Professional Advice: Consult with financial advisors for personalized advice.

A New Beginning

I will admit that my focus is to touch more lives, write a couple of books, get paid for training and consulting, invest in real estate, work with the right team of people, and equip people to win the right way. I am not going to lie; I would like all these things to happen very soon. But this year has taught me some life lessons, and I have also had some awakenings. I will share a few of these lessons with you.

Life Lesson #1: "Everything happens for a reason."

I got that quote from Lisa Nichols. Lisa will tell you that she got it from somewhere else; it did not originate from her. The year 2020 was one of the hardest for me and my parents. She stated that this statement helps you take the focus off your present situation. It also invites you to give up control, let go, and stop getting frustrated when things don't go your way. Try to see beyond the inconveniences, hurt, rejection, and pain, and learn that man's rejection might be God's way of blessing me. He might also be protecting me from something that could be even more harmful.

Life Lesson #2: Work on "Finding Your Niche."

The pandemic demonstrated how our jobs are not reliable. I think God wants me and his children to be self-sufficient (but not to the point where we become arrogant), crafty, or create our own products. Maybe even become self-made millionaires like Tyler Perry. Jesus was not just a minister of the gospel, but he was a businessman too. In John 4:4–26, He used the woman at the well to be his "Marketing Lady." After talking to her and reviewing her life story – she brought the whole town to come meet Him.

Life Lesson#3: The Road to Success Is Always Under Construction."

"The Road to Success Is Always Under Construction" is a metaphorical phrase that suggests success is not a destination but an ongoing journey. Success requires constant effort, learning, and improvement. There's always room to grow and new challenges to tackle. The path to success is not linear. It involves overcoming obstacles, adapting to changes, and navigating unexpected detours. Achieving success demands perseverance. There will be setbacks and failures, but maintaining the determination to keep going is crucial.

I hope this book has been helpful, encouraging, and a blessing to you. Thank you!

Tools and Resources

Aging Services Eldercare Locator

The first step to finding resources for older adults in the United States is	
800-677-1116 *www.eldercare.gov*	**Alzheimer's Association** 800-272-3900 *www.Alz.org*
Caregiver Support Groups	
AARP 1-888-687-2277 *www.aarp.org*	**Family Caregiver Alliance** 1-800-445-8106
Caregiver Action Network 202-454-3970	**Rosalynn Carter Institute for Caregiving** 229-928-1234
Senior Source 214-823-5700	
Dallas County Department of Health and Human Services	
Older Adult Services Program 214-819-1866	**Home Repair for Seniors** **Habitat for Humanity Greater Garland** 2909 Broadway Blvd., Garland, TX. 972-414-6894
Hearts and Hammers Senior Repair 651-636-0797 *info@heartsandhammers.org*	**City of Dallas Housing and Revitalization** *www.dallashousingpolicy.com*
Rebuilding Together Greater Dallas A national volunteer organization focused on the home repair and improvement needs of lower-income homeowners. 972-245-6900 800-473-4229 *www.rebuildingtogether.org*	

U.S. Department of Health and Human Services	
Administration on Aging *www.aoa.gov*	**Real Estate Services for Seniors** AW Real Estate Services 214-225-0757 *http://willisan.kw.com*

Real Estate Website and Channels	
http://www.willisan.kw.com http://www.YouTube.com/ Roadtoecoempwmt	**Business Sources** SCORE *www.score.org*
LIFTFUND *www.liftfund.com*	**DEC Network** *www.thedec.co*
SBA *www.Sba.gov*	

Miscellaneous	
Social Security Office 800-772-1213	**Dallas County Energy** Assistance (CEAP) 214-819-1848
City of Dallas Services 3-1-1	**Connect to Care Referrals for services** 888-743-1202
City of Dallas Office of Community Care/Senior Services 214-670-5227	**Legal Aid of NorthWest Texas** 214-748-1234
Mental Health America of Greater Dallas 214-871-2420	**Dental Health** N. Dallas Shared Ministries 214-358-8729
Dental Health Dr. M.C. Cooper Clinic 214-370-7260	**North Texas Food Bank** 214-330-1396
NTFB (PAN) 214-367-3123	

Caregiver Checklist	
Documents you need to help manage your recipient's finances *https://nfca.typepad.com/files/checklist.pdf*	

CHAPTER 14

Why should you join our community?

Over the years, Road to Economic Empowerment Enterprises has heard endless stories from those overwhelmed with caring for and paying for their elderly parents living expenses to those in the small business world struggling to grow their business. Successfully, Road to Economic Empowerment Enterprises has inspired some people to start their own business and offered solutions to help them better manage their finances, save thousands of dollars on senior living expenses, and more. If you need a little extra support in creating SMART Goals for your circumstances, business, aging loved one, or just looking for a way to make new friends, our Road to Economic Empowerment Community is the right place for you. We partner with other non-profits as well as those in the business community to provide personal and professional development training. One thing we know is that no one can do this life alone. No matter what road or journey you are on. Be it the road to success or otherwise.

Here are a few more reasons why you should join:

- We partner and coordinate services with professional experts in the real estate, credit, law, health, and non-medical industries.
- We offer over 15 years of experience in real estate and public services.
- We believe that investing in human capital is a company's greatest asset.
- We put our members in the driver's seat to make them feel important.
- We give back through community outreach.
- Members will receive free service coordination with startup, financial, legal, and mental health support organizations and affiliates.
- Members will get a free vision board planner and goal worksheet, a book or journal, and maybe even a plan of action session to help them find their niche. We will assign an accountability partner once we devise a plan of action.
- Members will receive discounts on books, masterclasses, and events.

Our Purpose:

The purpose of the Road to Economic Empowerment Community is to provide a platform or space for members to experience holistic growth and empowerment.

The focus areas of Road to Economic Empowerment Enterprises:

- Homeownership
- Financial literacy and wealth-building
- Empowerment through education
- Community Impact and Social Change
- Caregiver Support and Resources
- Youth mentorship and development
- Networking and Collaboration
- Health and Wellness

Each mindset session includes group discussions, workshops, and action planning to ensure members leave with tangible steps to implement what they have learned.

Join our

R2EE ENTERPRISE COMMUNITY

Over the years, Road to Economic Empowerment Enterprises has heard endless stories from those overwhelmed with caring for and paying for their elderly parents living expenses to those in the small business world struggling to grow their business. Successfully, Road to Economic Empowerment Enterprises has inspired some people to start their own business, offered solutions to help them better manage their finances, save thousands of dollars on senior living expenses, and more. If you need a little extra support in creating SMART Goals for your circumstances, business, aging loved one, or just looking for a way to make new friends our Road to Economic Empowerment Community is the right place for you. We partner with other non profits as well as those in the business community to provide personal and professional development training. One thing we know is that NO ONE CAN DO THIS LIFE ALONE. No matter what road or journey you are on. Be it the road to success or otherwise.

Online
SMART GOALS MASTER CLASS

MY PROGRAM PLA

$197 $197

r SMART Goals course and learn how to plan of action to help you achieve your d or professional goals more clearly. efficiently, and succinctly.

LET'S DO IT

GISTRATION LINK IN BIO

SIGN UP NOW

Frequently Asked Questions

1. Where do you meet?

A: Our YouTube channel, www.YouTube.com/roadtoecoempwmt, has all of our past and current trainings.

We are currently working on setting up a membership on our channel, or LMS platform, where our masterclasses and meetups will be for private members only. More details are coming soon.

2. How often do you meet?

A: Depending upon the group size, schedule, and other factors, the groups will meet biweekly or monthly to discuss challenges, set goals, and track progress.

3. What do you all do during your meetings?

A: Members usually share their goals or interests, which can range from business growth, personal development, or specific projects.

4. Do members hold each other accountable?

A: Currently, we do not. Once we set up our mastermind group, its primary function will be to hold each member accountable for their goals and commitments.

5. Is your Road to Economic Empowerment Community a safe space?

A: Yes, our trainings and meetups are a safe space where members can share their challenges and successes without fear of judgment, fostering mutual support and encouragement.

6. What does it cost to join?

A: Currently, it is free, but that will soon change.

7. Are you all looking for community and business partners?

A: Yes, we are looking for successful business owners, leaders, and community partners to provide mentorship and strategies. Facilitators are also needed to facilitate mastermind meetups and training.

8. How can future business partners, volunteers, and members reach a representative?

A: They can reach out to Angela Willis at 214-225-0757 or email us at info@r2eeEnterprise.org.

What values does the non-profit uphold, and do you have any testimonials?

Our Values:

- We love openness and clarity
- We are driven by respect
- We try to see things through the eyes of others
- We practice listening, learning & humility
- We love a caring & an exuberating personality
- We support cultural diversity & inclusion- fostering racially and economically diverse communities
- We value practicing self-care

Testimonials

"Hi Angie! I was going to wait until we actually see something but couldn't wait to tell you that my mom called today crying because she was happy that VA determined her husband has 80% disability. You have made a difference in their quality of life and now hopefully giving their family some financial relief and Ben her husband can proudly say I'm a veteran without crying in shame. They are honoring him now. A Huge thank you!" - **Daion C.**

_____

"It is always great to be around people who ambitious and strive for greatness. You have awesome energy, and I can tell you love people and enjoy life." - **Greg Hall, Allegiance Title**

_____

"I was inspired to go back to school and get my braiding license because of the seminar hosted by Angela Willis" - **Sakina Glenn, Founder of The Secret Place NineONE:1**

Road to Economic Empowerment Enterprises Past Classes and Seminars

MAY 2019

The Cost of Caregiving: Alzheimer's and Caregivers Financial Health Symposium

Partners and Speakers:

Attorney Michael Cohen, Michael B. Cohen Law Firm
Angela Hodges, Alzheimer's Association

MAY 2018

The Cost of Caregiving: Alzheimer's and Caregivers (FH)

Partners: Alzheimer's Association, and Sponsors:

PC Home Health and Friends Place in DeSoto
Speakers: Rebecca Williams, Mr. Toliver, and James Henderson

MARCH 2017

The Cost of Caregiving: Alzheimer's and Caregivers Financial Health Symposium

Partners: Sweet Fellowship Family Center

Friends Place
Dallas Area Agency on Aging
Author of "Path to Peace," Angie Jones

MARCH 2016

Get Financially Fit Part II: "Tax Strategies"
Partner: Sheila Lofton

MARCH 2015

Get Financially Fit: "Budgeting and Credit Improvement"
Partner: Transformance

NOVEMBER 2014

Can You Help a Sista or Brotha Out Lunch n Learn
Partner: Cassandra Bradford

JULY 2014

Financial Education Seminar: "It's Only a Matter of Time

Partners:

Sheila Lofton, CEO of S.G. Lofton & Associates, and Tarsha Polk, CEO of "The Marketing Lady."

ANGELA WILLIS

Angela is passionately dedicated to educating leaders and serving the community. She founded Road to Economic Empowerment Enterprises, a 501(c)(3) non-profit, and owns Road to Economic Empowerment Training and Events along with AW Real Estate Group. She is a highly sought-after Master Your Mindset Empowerment Leadership Trainer, Author, and Realtor, and her primary mission is to help leaders positively transform their work or living environments through her empowerment books, trainings, and real estate services.

With a strong educational background in Human Resources Management, a master's degree in management, and over fifteen years of experience in criminal justice and sales, Angela has influenced and inspired over 2,000 troubled youth and countless adults. Her belief in leading by example drives her passion for making a difference. Angela, through her 501(c)(3) non-profit, Road to Economic Empowerment Enterprises, collaborates with other non-profits and those in the business community to empower underserved communities. The organization offers personal and professional development in entrepreneurship, financial literacy, affordable housing education, and mental health wellness advocacy. Some have compared the organization to being like SCORE, but with a financial twist.

CONTACT US

7200 W. University Drive Suite 300
Mckinney, TX 75071
Office: (214) 225 - 0757
info@r2eeenterprise.org